W9-BVC-601

MEET ROSA PARKS

MELODY S. MIS

PowerKiDS
press.

New York

To Clara Raben—your book at last

Published in 2008 by The Rosen Publishing Group, Inc.
29 East 21st Street, New York, NY 10010

Copyright © 2008 by The Rosen Publishing Group, Inc.

All rights reserved. No part of this book may be reproduced in any form without permission in writing from the publisher, except by a reviewer.

First Edition

Editor: Nicole Pristash and Jennifer Way
Book Design: Julio Gil
Photo Researcher: Nicole Pristash

Photo Credits: Cover Library of Congress Prints and Photographs Division; back cover, title page, headers, pp. 9, 17, 19 © Getty Images; p. 5 © Paul Schutzer/Getty Images; p. 7 © Ed Clark/Getty Images; p. 11 © Francis Miller/Getty Images; pp. 13, 15 © Don Cravens/Getty Images; p. 21 © Associated Press.

Library of Congress Cataloging-in-Publication Data

Mis, Melody S.
   Meet Rosa Parks / by Melody S. Mis. — 1st ed.
      p. cm. — (Civil rights leaders)
   Includes bibliographical references and index.
   ISBN 978-1-4042-4210-4 (library binding)
   1. Parks, Rosa, 1913–2005—Juvenile literature. 2. African Americans—Alabama—Montgomery—Biography—Juvenile literature. 3. African American civil rights workers—Alabama—Montgomery—Biography—Juvenile literature. 4. Civil rights workers—Alabama—Montgomery—Biography—Juvenile literature. 5. Montgomery (Ala.)—Biography—Juvenile literature. 6. Montgomery Bus Boycott, Montgomery, Ala., 1955–1956—Juvenile literature. 7. Segregation in transportation—Alabama—Montgomery—History—20th century—Juvenile literature. 8. African Americans—Civil rights—Alabama—Montgomery—Juvenile literature. 9. Montgomery (Ala.)—Race relations—Juvenile literature. I. Title.
   F334.M753P38557 2008
   323.092—dc22
   [B]
                                        2007034840

Manufactured in the United States of America

Contents

In December 1955, Rosa Parks was riding the bus home from work. When the bus driver told her to give her seat to a white man, Parks said, "No." She was tired of being treated unfairly because she was black. She believed she had the same right to sit down as the white man did.

Parks's choice to stand up for her rights was an important moment in the United States' history. It marked the beginning of the **civil rights movement**. The civil rights movement was a period of time when people worked toward getting equal rights for African Americans.

Rosa Parks helped change many lives. Her hard work led to peace and equality for many African Americans.

Rosa McCauley was born on February 4, 1913, in Tuskegee, Alabama. At a young age, she moved and grew up on her grandparents' farm in Pine Level, Alabama.

The first school Rosa attended was for black people. It was a one-room schoolhouse. At that time, African Americans and whites could not go to the same school. This was because of **segregation**. Unlike white children, black children went to school five months a year. They had to work on farms the rest of the year. After age 11, Rosa went to school in Montgomery, Alabama. She left high school at 16 to take care of her sick grandmother.

During segregation, black children could not go to the same schools as white children. Many black children had to go to a one-room schoolhouse, like this one.

The Jim Crow South

During the first half of Parks's life, people in the South were segregated because of the Jim Crow laws. These laws said that whites and blacks should be kept apart but treated the same. Sadly, this did not happen. Whites treated many black people unfairly.

Under Jim Crow laws, African Americans could not vote. Blacks and whites had to go to different schools. They had different bathrooms in public places. African Americans had to sit in the back rows of public buses. If a bus was full, drivers made blacks give up their seats to whites and ride standing up.

The Ku Klux Klan, or KKK, is a group of white men who are against African-American equality. The KKK used to wear white sheets so people would not know who they were. They burned crosses in front of African Americans' homes. Sometimes, they beat up blacks and burned their churches.

COLORED

This African-American boy is drinking from a water fountain that only black people could use. This was very common in the South during segregation.

In 1932, Rosa married Raymond Parks and moved to Montgomery, Alabama. She went back to high school and finished two years later. This was important because at that time, only 7 out of 100 African Americans finished high school.

Rosa Parks wanted to change the way African Americans were treated. In 1943, she joined the National Association for the Advancement of Colored People, or the NAACP. The NAACP worked to get equal rights for blacks. Rosa began working there. She helped blacks sign up to vote and took children to see the Freedom Train.

The Freedom Train was a real train that traveled around the country. The people on the train taught visitors about the rights they had as Americans.

This man is visiting the Freedom Train during its first year, in 1947. The Freedom Train helped many blacks see that they should have the same rights as white people.

On December 1, 1955, Parks left work and got on the bus to go home. She sat in the area for blacks. After the bus filled up, a white man was left standing. The bus driver told Parks to get up so the white man could sit. Bus drivers were not supposed to make riders sitting in the black section move when there were no other empty seats. Most drivers did not follow this rule, though. Parks felt that this was wrong.

Parks refused to move out of her seat. She felt she should be able to sit down, too. The bus driver got angry. He called the police, who came and **arrested** Parks.

The black part of a bus was generally in the back or middle, where Parks (right) is sitting. Sometimes, blacks were not even allowed to use the front door.

When blacks in Montgomery heard about Parks's arrest, they **protested** against it. Martin Luther King Jr., a civil rights leader, asked them to **boycott** the bus company. This meant they would not ride the city buses and the company would lose a lot of money. King hoped that a peaceful boycott would make the company stop practicing segregation.

Many African Americans in Montgomery did not ride the buses for a year. They shared rides or walked to work. This was hard on many of them. Some had to walk 12 miles (19 km). Finally, the government forced the bus company to end segregation. This was a great accomplishment.

14

Martin Luther King Jr., shown here, is planning the bus boycott with Rosa Parks and other leaders in 1956.

Many white people in Montgomery blamed Rosa for the bus boycott. She and her husband lost their jobs. Some people even said they wanted to hurt or kill her. Rosa and Raymond decided to move north to Detroit, Michigan, in 1957. They believed they would be safer there.

In 1965, Parks went to work for an African American named John Conyers Jr. He was a civil rights leader and worked for the U.S. government. Parks and Conyers did great things together. They worked to get housing for poor African Americans throughout the city. Parks worked in Conyers's office until 1988.

Blacks in Detroit were tired of being treated poorly. They started a riot in 1967. This means they destroyed parts of the city (shown here) out of anger.

Raymond Parks died in 1977. To honor him, Rosa started the Rosa and Raymond Parks **Institute** for Self-Development. The institute teaches young African Americans how they can help others in their neighborhoods and cities.

One of the programs the Parks Institute runs is called Pathways to Freedom. It sends high-school students on bus trips. They go to places that are important to African-American history and the civil rights movement. The students learn about the hard and unsafe work that many people did to help African Americans gain equal rights and their freedom from **slavery**.

From the 1600s to the 1800s, slavery existed in the United States. This means that some white people owned black people and forced them to work for no pay. Some brave people helped slaves escape by feeding and hiding them. This was called the Underground Railroad.

18

These schoolchildren are visiting the bus on which Rosa Parks stood up for her rights. It is located at the Henry Ford Museum, in Dearborn, Michigan.

During her life, Parks received many **awards** for her work for civil rights and peace. She was given two of the United States' highest honors. In 1996, she received the **Medal** of Freedom. Three years later, Parks received the Congressional Gold Medal. Only 250 people have been given this award.

These awards show how important Parks was to African-American history and the civil rights movement. If Parks had not stood up for her rights that day on the bus, segregation may not have ended so soon.

In 1997, Rosa Parks was given the Lifetime Achievement Award by the American Public Transit Association.

Parks died in Detroit on October 24, 2005, at age 92. She was taken to Montgomery, Alabama, where a special church service was held for her. Afterward, Parks was taken to the U.S. Capitol building in Washington, D.C. Thousands of people passed by her **casket** to honor her. She was buried beside her husband in Detroit.

Parks is often called the mother of the civil rights movement. She fought against unfair laws and helped end segregation in the South. Today, the Parks Institute teaches young people about the importance of her work and the civil rights movement.

Glossary

arrested (uh-REST-ed) Stopped from doing a crime.

awards (uh-WORDZ) Special honors given to someone.

boycott (BOY-kot) To join with others in refusing to buy from or deal with a business.

casket (KAS-ket) A long box that holds a dead person who is to be buried.

civil rights (SIH-vul RYTS) The rights that citizens have.

institute (IN-stih-toot) A place or group that aids a certain cause.

medal (MEH-dul) A small, round object that is given as a prize.

movement (MOOV-ment) A group of people who get together to back the same cause or purpose.

protested (pruh-TEST-ed) Acted out in disagreement of something.

segregation (seh-gruh-GAY-shun) The act of keeping people of one race, gender, or class apart from others.

slavery (SLAY-vuh-ree) The system of one person owning another.

Index

Web Sites

Due to the changing nature of Internet links, PowerKids Press has developed an online list of Web sites related to the subject of this book. This site is updated regularly. Please use this link to access the list:
www.powerkidslinks.com/crl/rosa/